Wit
More
Help
From My Friends

by

Elizabeth Fleming

E. ᴧᴧ

A Sea Minor Publication

ISBN-13: 978-1494254353

ISBN-10: 1494254352

This second book is dedicated to 3 very
special people:

MY MUM AND DAD WHO ARE NO
LONGER WITH US

and my

DEAREST FRIEND MAUREEN

WHO PASSED AWAY

DECEMBER 2011

With A Little *More* Help From My Friends

Foreword

The story told by Elizabeth Fleming in her first book is one of inspiration, allowing the reader to watch on as a doctor sent to declare her dead shortly after her birth noticed a tiny flicker of life. From that point we were able to follow an account of her developing and flourishing against all the odds. It tells of the overcoming of many of the obstacles placed in her way by her Cerebral Palsy and of the crucial role her family and friends played in her this tale.

As a title for that first book, I toyed with the idea of using 'Walking With Lazarus'. It seemed apt.

In this, her second book, you'll find that the trials and tribulations of Elizabeth's early years were only hinted at in her debut. It tells of the struggle of a human being to cope with some of the natural disasters of life.

As we watch Elizabeth cope with the tragedy of cancer in her family, we get a real sense of her emotional pain. She's removed from her environment, first of all by medication and then because of the effects the medication had on her. Two-and-a-half years of her adulthood were spent within the confines of a psychiatric hospital where she came to terms with waves of trauma we can only imagine. The story reminded me of Ken Casey's classic tale and I was tempted to use the title 'Another One Flew Over The Cuckoo's Nest'; when I read on about the role of therapists, medical staff and those close to her and watched her emerge from her cocoon once more, there was only one title I could use:

With A Little More Help From My Friends.

The sequel takes the first story and simply raises the stakes.

If you were inspired by Elizabeth's faith and tenacity in her first book, I can assure you that you ain't seen nothing yet

Follow on story

It is January the 7th 2012 as I sit at 6.00pm ready to begin the next part of my story. I was lucky in December 2011 to have the first part published as an E-book. Everyone keeps asking about the next part, so at the start of this New Year I have decided to begin.

The last time I wrote about myself I was only 28 years old. I am now 46. 18 years have passed and so much has happened. I wish now I had kept notes, as trying to think back as it is not as easy as it once was.

Elizabeth Fleming

Chapter 1

It is hard to think back all those year ago, so I will start from August 1999.

One evening my mum and dad were going to see a film at the cinema. They were going up to see a popular film at that time. On the way to the film my mum was walking along when suddenly she fell and went tumbling down. She got up quickly but she really got a sore one. They never got to see the film as Dad had to bring her home. Back home I ran her a hot bath but it was plain to see she had hurt herself badly. Mum being Mum, she tried to not make a fuss, but this fall was to change all of our lives forever.

Eventually, after much persuading, Mum was forced to go to her GP. She had broken three ribs and was severely bruised. We had to take turns helping her in and out of the bath. I hated seeing her in so much pain. By November, Mum was having tests, and a scan was given. To everyone's shock the diagnosis was lung cancer.

The doctor reckoned it was her fall and when she broke his ribs it punctured her lung. The cancer could have been lying dormant for years but the rib punctured Mum's lung which upset the cancer. Mum was to start treatment in the New Year.

As I sit writing this it seems so long ago. Do I really want to remember the past and all the pain and sadness? And this is only the first chapter. I really want to try because of the feedback from my first book. It's not going to be an easy road. It's never been easy from day one, but I hope I find the courage to complete it, as I think it will be worth it in the end

As the millennium approached, we all sat as a large family to bring in the New Year. There were Mum, Dad, Diane, John, Moira, Derek, Ina, Johnny, John's parents, four children and me. This was sadly to be the last time we were all together. We were all so happy just spending family time with each other.

Chapter 2

At the start of 2000 we knew that my mum was to face radio-therapy. The tests had revealed that the lung cancer was in one part of her lung only. At first everything seemed quite positive. The surgeon thought removing the lung was the right way to go. But Mum had many health problems and at this time another doctor said surgery was too risky so they opted for Radical Radium.

It was very hard to come to terms with this as a close family. My mum was the head of our family. She was very kind and gentle and she guided us through our lives. The thought of not having her was too hard to imagine. How could I not have Mum around?

My life at this point was just the same. I still worked at the nursery. We tried hard to live as normal day-to-day lives as we could. Dad just kept saying Mum would be fine, but Dad always looked on the bright side of life and so did I at that stage. Mum was very positive and tried hard not to show Dad - and I how hard it was. Diane and Moira were a great help and support to Mum. They helped her though her hospital appointments and treatment. Dad did his bit the best he could. I did not travel in buses and cars then, but I was there to help and take care of mum after her treatment.

The person I was then and the person I am today are so different. You will read how I change. If only things had been different, then I could have been more help. Mum worried from the day I took my first breath about how I would manage and how my life might turn out.

Mum's treatment went ahead in March. It was hard going as she had five treatments a week. It only lasted for a few minutes each time, but the toing and froing ever day was hard. She just slept in the car as the treatment exhausted her. But it would all be worth it if it worked. My mum's treatment seemed to work and once she recovered, things got back to normal for a while.

After she recovered, my dad decided to send Mum, Moira and Diane to Tenerife. I could have gone, but I still suffered from panic attacks. If only I had been the person I have now become. I would have loved to have gone. My panic attacks ruined so much of my life then, and sadly I can't turn the clock back. But we all have regrets in our lives.

About the May of that year, my brother-in-law's mum, Ina, was beginning to feel ill. Ina was just a lovely sweet lady who loved being part of a big family. All Ina worried about was John's dad.

Johnny was a diabetic and did not keep well. My dad and Johnny were dog men. As the months progressed, we found out that Ina had cancer of the blood. Things were hard as John, my brother in-law, was an only son. I was only 12 when Diane and John started to date and John's parents just loved having girls about the place. Diane and John had made plans to take the children to Florida in August of that year. It had been booked for almost 2 years. Could they go away for 3 week knowing that Ina was poorly and Johnny's health was not good? Ross and Nicky had been so excited for so long and were at the right age to appreciate the holiday. We all, as a family wanted, them to go and Mum, Dad, Moira, Derek and I said we would help out to let the Gordons have their family holiday

Ina and Jonny were just so lovely, although Johnny could be difficult at times, but he was a man after all. Diane, John and the children got their holiday, but not long after they returned Johnny died.

The funny thing was I could see John's dad going down and I kept saying to my mum I think Johnny will go first. My mum said it was nonsense, and reminded me that it was Ina who was ill. I just knew and it was so unlike me to predict anything but I was right. Sadly Ina died three months after that in the December.

It had been a hard year for the family. Mum's

cancer and John losing his parents. Ina just got cremated during the Christmas week, so that Christmas we decided to have Christmas with our own families. We just felt it was too soon to celebrate anything. It was very sad and we said we hoped we'd never have it without each other again.

Chapter 3

My mum had a full year of good health and looking back now, we all made the most of it. Sadly, however, she became unwell early in 2001. This time was so hard as things just did not look good. My mum and dad were to celebrate their 65th birthdays in June of that year. My sisters and I decided to organise a surprise party for them. We are a very close family and quite private, but we just wanted to give them a party. It was hard as we share everything with each other. But somehow we managed to keep it a secret. We managed to get them to the party and, boy, did it go with a bang. My mum's face was a picture. Afterwards my mum and dad said it was the best present they had ever received.

As I write this the tears are running down my face. It is so hard, but uplifting to be reminded of all these years ago. It just seems so far away and so much has changed since. But no one can ever take all those memories away.

The party was the last time my mum saw most of her friends. After that her health deteriorated. The months that followed were painful and heart breaking. The cancer had returned but it was more aggressive this time. They decided to remove Mum's lung this time. But sadly with Mum's poor health it was impossible for her to return to normal health. After her operation she returned home. She was on oxygen but she was such a fighter, still trying to look on the positive side.

At home we tried to carry on with our lives. Although I saw how ill Mum was, never for one minute did I think she was going to die. Looking back I wonder how I never realised what was happening. People say you don't when it is someone so close to you. Mum took a stroke and after her stroke my Mum returned home. I still had never been in to visit as at that stage. I never went in the car for long journeys. I was so scared I did not want Mum home. I felt so bad afterwards as Mum wanted to return home to be with her family. But once I saw her I was fine. Although very ill underneath, she was still that wonderful person we all loved dearly. Three day after Mum came home she slipped into a coma and die with her family beside her. We had had carers round the clock but Mum's last wish was to have just her family who meant the world to her by her side and we managed to give her that wish.

The tears have started again. O how I wonder if I will ever get it finished and if you, the reader, will be crying too.

The following days were just like a daze. Family and friends coming and going, the kettle never off. Diane and I had to go down to the bank to do some business. As we were going down to the bank, we met a friend of Mum's and what she said stuck in my mind. She said how are you? Are you over her death yet? We just did not answer her and walked on. How could we be over Mum's death. What strange thing to say?

My Mum was the most important person in my life. People say time is a great healer and, yes, it eases the pain a little. But there is a part of me that did not want to accept she had gone. That might have been why it took me so long, as you will learn later, to come to terms with her death. As I write today it is 10 years since Mum's death and there is not one day since then that me or my sisters have not thought or talked about her, and I hope we always do. You only get one Mum and Dad and Diane, Moira and I were so lucky to have had them.

Ross, Nicky, Julie and Kristy were trying so hard to be brave, but it was so soon after Ian and Johnny had died. It was tough on everyone. Seeing the children all in black was so sad. They were still very young. Ross, 15, Julie and Nicky 13 and Kristy just 11. They had lost someone so dear. Mum just loved being a granny. Before Mum had died she said to Ross, please look after Aunty Bibby for me. Here come the tears, and from that day forward he has kept to his word. The funeral was just a daze. It sounds silly but I can only remember a bit of that day. Walking into church with Ross by my side, seeing the church full of people but hardly recognizing any one, picking my school friends from primary out and walking home with my family from the tea. The rest was blur. I have often tried to fill in the gaps but for some reason I have never been able to.

Chapter 4

After Mum's death, my family just tried hard to get on with life. Again, I can't remember much about the first 7 weeks. I felt I had to just get on and take care of the running of the house and looking after Dad. Mum had been the organiser. She ran the house and paid the bills, so that became my role. I did not cry much after Mum's death. I just bottled it up inside. After 5 weeks, one day I just could not stop shaking. My dad called the GP and he thought it was just me grieving. The GP gave me Diazepam. My Dad has been on this medication for many years and Dad was convinced that this would help. But this was the beginning of a three year battle with drugs, mental-health problems, and 2 years 8 months in a hospital.

The medication did not work and I was just getting worse by the day. I just shook inside and after 7 weeks I became violent. I was lashing out at my family as the feelings inside my tummy were so bad. My Dad kept telling me to take another tablet so it would pass. My family had to call the police as I was screaming for my mum. The police came, and had no choice but to take me up to a police station in Edinburgh and put me in a cell. They took my picture I can still see the photo in my head. The police said if I did not settle down this was where I would end up. I was so frightened as I just did not know what was happening to me. Sitting in a cell for 2 hours, with men shouting and swearing. The police then took me home.

This is the first time in 10 years I have been able to tell anyone this. I don't even think my sisters knew what had happened that night. Although I think I told my social worker 2 years later. I was so scared to admit to telling anyone because of the fear it might happen again.

The following morning I was still very agitated and John took me for a walk near my house until it was time for me to go into the local psychiatric hospital. It was there I was to spend the next year of my life. Unknown to me at this time, the Diazepam I was prescribed should never been given to someone with Cerebral Palsy.

At first I was allowed visitors. I was so hopped up with medication I hardly knew what day it was. I just asked for more and more medication and at first they gave me it. Everyone came in from home, my family nearly every day, my church friends and work friends. There was very little help and all we did was sit about looking at four walls, or sat in the sunshine. I spent most of my days on a bench sleeping my life away. My family was in bits and my life was falling apart and no one could help me. After a time I was allowed home for day passes but sadly they failed and I became more violent and distressed. What a waste of a year of life. I walked round and round the Hospital grounds in my own wee world. It's scary thinking about this now, but it did get better, but it was a long hard and lonely road that lay ahead of me.

Before this happened I had lived a normal life. I had Cerebral Palsy but my mum and dad decided to treat me just the same as my sisters. I never felt different at home although I was spoilt, but I *was* the baby of the family after all.

As a child I got angry and frustrated but nothing like the violent person I had become. The violence became uncontrollable and I was shifted to secure units all around the country. Unknown to me but they talked about taking me down to London to try and get me the help I needed. Although at that time no one knew what to do with me. Then one day two people from the Royal Edinburgh Hospital came to asses me. Unknown to me at the time, the lady I will call L, was to be one of the main people who helped me to get my new life back together again.

My head was so mixed up. I only get flashbacks of things. But I remember L giving me blocks to work out and I could not do them, then I took 'a turn'

which we called them later and that was the end of
another assessment. After a year in Haddington I
was transferred to the Robert Ferguson Unit in
Edinburgh.

Chapter 5

At this stage I was nearly unrecognizable. I had lost
so much weight. I was like a skeleton. My life was
just a living hell. I had my own room and in
between my violent turns I just stayed in my room.
I just did not want to go on and wanted to die. I
was hurting myself. I tried anything I could to get
out of the hell hole I was living in. I spent so much
time by myself. I had no idea where I was, or really
didn't care as the medication had blocked
everything out. I never cried or grieved for my
mum for nearly 18 months.

At this stage my family was told it would be very
unlikely that I would make a full recovery and live a
normal life again. That, my sisters say, was the
hardest thing to take on board. How could they
have had a sister who had lived a normal life turn
out so different? Diane and Moira said it was like I
had died because for so long I was out of their
lives.

I had no visits from home. I never saw my family
or friends for almost a year. But to be honest I
never missed them as I was so ill. It's funny,

though, that I always prayed each night that one day I would return home again, but I did not think it could happen. I was so ill that getting better seemed too far and hard to achieve. The unit seemed to always be busy throughout the day. It had people coming and going all day long. The Nurses checked on me all the time. I was not getting medication on demand when I asked for it which made me lash out even more.

Why was I doing all these things? I was not stupid. I knew that you did not behave in this way. It was the feelings inside me, they were so powerful and painful it was so unbearable. The agitation inside got to a point that I had to hurt myself or lash out to get rid of the pain. At one point I looked like a boxer. I was black and blue. What a mess. Where did it all go so wrong?

Lying in that small room day in day out was horrible. Was this to be my life forever more? Surely not.

The staff would talk to me in the dining room. Asking me what was going on in my head. The funny thing is I can only remember bits and pieces of this time. It was as if I was just living in my own wee world. I was terrified to be near another human being in case I took a turn. Imagine me being scared of being beside someone.

At my lowest point, my next step would have been to be sent to a woman's prison. I was so scared and low I just wanted to die. The charge nurse was called L. She tried so hard to talk to me. She was just lovely I was to learn later.

Eventually the staff had to get me out of that room. The unit was just like a long corridor. It was so scary. I was to be out of my room for just a short time each day, then longer and longer until I felt comfortable. How would I manage this? It was so hard. I had lost all my confidence. When I think back, I felt as though I had died and step by step and day by day I was learning to live again. I sat up at the end of the unit, still by myself, but people could come up and talk to me. What must everyone have thought of me? A horror on legs. I tried to sneak back into my room but it was locked. They had me well sussed out.

At my lowest point I weight 4 stone 3lb. I was so thin nothing fitted me. I was thin as a child, but as a teenager and woman I was small made but chubby. I hardly recognised myself. I felt it was a shame because I was so ill I did not enjoy being thin. My family were told that I would probably never lead a normal life again and would spend the rest of my life in hospital.

One day, a male nurse call J, took me for a walk round the hospital. I wonder if he remembers what he said to me? I used to be horrible to him and he was so nice, but they all were after a while. He said that one day I would really like this L therapist and she and I would be a good team and she would help me in so many ways if I just let her. At that stage I thought I'd never like her. To me she was a monster who was making me do things I did not want to do. She will recognise herself if she reads this.

Chapter 6

Day by day and week by week things did improve, but very slowly and coming out of my room got easier and easier. The unit was a specialist place. Unknown to me at the time, every day you got your own nurse who looked after you. The nurses were just great; very kind and understanding. What must they have thought of me? I used to think I was just a horror but afterwards I realised it was part of my illness. I knew there was a nice me waiting to come out, but how would I show myself to everyone.

   After coming out of my room, the next step was to interact with people again. This was so hard because I was still scared of taking a turn. L and I talked about this and worked out what was happening. So again, bit by bit, I started to mix with people on the unit. I had it up and down, good times and not so good times, but it was a start for me on that long road to the new me.

   In the unit you had your own Therapist for everything. You had your own Psychologist, Speech Therapist, Art Therapist, Three OTs,

Physiotherapist, Social Workers, Consultant, a lady Doctor and the nurses. So many people to get to know and for me to trust, but again bit by bit day by day it was happening.

The nurses were just so nice and kind towards all the patients. There were so many and they all cared for you equally. There were a few very special nurses who I grew very fond of. But at this time I still had no contact with family or home. Gilly, MB, JL, JG and G were very important to me.

When I was very unwell. JL would come and talk to me and tell me that things would get better and that there was a light at the end of my tunnel. She would pray with me at times which helped my keep my faith going. My faith was a big challenge for me at that time. Where was God when I needed him so much? But he was there. I just had to look harder for him then.

It was now time to face my biggest fear of all - going outside. But every new step I made was scary at first. But again we tackled it step by step. The unit had now become safe. I no longer dreaded seeing people I was familiar with. That was except for L. Poor L. She was my Mrs Bossy Boots. I never told her this but every time I saw her coming my heart would race and she was not always coming up to see me. I am going to keep you wondering for a wee bit longer to see how L and I finished up.

CHAPTER 7

The outside world seemed a scary place for someone who had been in hospital for so long. L and I made a plan. We were only going out for 2 minutes and then back in, but boy was it scary. We did this every day, five days a week at the same time but longer each time. I tried every trick in the book not to go but L was not having any of my nonsense. I felt physically sick each time, but L kept insisting and after I did it I was so proud of myself, until the next day when L would be up for our walk. Gilly and nurse G helped out when they were on shift.

One day I was out with L and I just wanted to take her arm, but could I dare ask her? After all, she was a psychologist. So I plucked up the courage and she said of course I could. Could this L person be nice after all I wondered? My dream, for some reason, was to make it to the yellow bin. The yellow bin was quite far away from the unit in those early days. If I could make it there I could do anything, I thought. The day I reached that bin was a milestone and after that things just got better and better. And yes I even started to like L after all. L was the main person that pushed me to eventually being the independent person I have now become.

Bit by bit, piece by piece, things were getting better. I was now working hard with every therapist. It was hard but the hard work was paying off.

The next step was making contact with home. For some reason I was scared they did not want me back. But unknown to me, the unit kept my sisters updated week by week. Again L and H, a student, made a plan. Although things were getting better I still had my hard days. The first time my sisters came in it went well. Sadly, on the second visit it did not. My poor sisters went away broken-hearted. I cried all weekend. L came in on Monday morning. I was so down and scared to face L again. But I had to face up to what had happened. I did, and once again we faced it and worked it through. Would Diane and Moira ever want to come back? I had to call them and say I was sorry and ask would they came again.

Thinking as I write today it all seems so long ago. How hard it is to be reminded of the bad bits. Back then I blamed myself, but I now know it was not all my fault. Medication can play a big part in anyone's life. If it is wrongly giving it can be very harmful.

My dear sisters did come back and with L's help it

did go well. I was back on the upward step again and it felt so good. My dad was still to be tackled. I think I even saw Mary before my dad.

I feel so sad, but I resented my dad because I so much wanted my mum back. My dad suffered for many years with nerves and depression. The medication that helped him was the medication that did not help me. I felt my dad would be the hardest to get to know again, and he was.

I was making steady progress. Everyone was happy and so was I. The unit was getting to see the nice me and I think they were quite surprised. I worked with A, the speech and language therapist. I found speech therapy hard. It was hard for me. Why did I need this - I thought my speech was fine. My sisters said that my speech was so much better, so it must have worked after all. A was lovely although that was the hardest thing I had to do.

Then there were A and B the OTs. We did a small group three mornings a week. We made files for hospitals. You got pocket money for helping. It kept me in sweets. They were just so nice. Then I worked with D, another OT. Once a week we would do shopping and cook. At first D would go and buy the food, but his bigger plan was for me and D to buy the food together, and again this challenge was achieved. I also had art therapy which I so much enjoyed. Why was I very surprised about that?

Then last, but by no means least came B. He was

my Social worker. When I first worked with a new person, L by now who I thought was just the nicest person in the place, would come until I knew the other person a little. B and I got on so well. He helped me so much when I was making the transfer from unit to home.

It's funny how thing change. As my treatment progressed and I started to look up to L, I thought of how did I not like the person at first. She was just so helpful and kind and only wanted to get me back on the right road.

Growing up I always felt very resentful to the people who wanted to help me. Did I resent being disabled? Yes. But no one ever spoke to me as a person. I was just my Mum's child. Professional people, doctors etc, never told me why they were poking and prodding me. But there I was being treated as a person at last and having to make my own decisions. It was so unusual. I never made a decision up until that point.

Mum was always there to take over my life, not in a nasty way, and if I could have her back I would but sadly that's not possible. Oh how much I miss her wee face. She was just the most precious person I ever had. I will have to stop now as I can't see for tears. Will I ever finish this book?

Chapter 8

Then came my Dad, I was doing well but I still had not had a lot of contact with Dad. I knew I had to get back to us having a daughter/father relationship. My dad wanted me to go to Tranent and see him, which was fine, but I so much wanted him to come to the unit into my world and meet the people I had been with for so long.

Again we did it step by step, but because I had not been out of Morningside I had no way of knowing where I was. The first time we just drove to Tranent and L, D and I and had a look round the town. Being away for nearly 2 years, things looked different. I took L and D round the places I knew. We never visited anybody the first time. It felt good seeing places that were familiar to me and showing my friends where I belonged. I know that they were my therapists, but they had also become my friends. I wondered what it would feel like to see where I had spent my life. Would I feel as if I belonged and would I want to return one day?

I was now texting my sisters on a daily basis. The second visit home, I went into my dad's house. He looked nervous, but happy to see me. It had been almost a year since I'd seen him. It was my home for so many years. How would I feel seeing things again?

It felt funny but in a nice way. My room still looked the same and my stuffed animals lay where they had been for 2 years. It was so nice sharing memories with L. My visit was timed as before, but we were over my time as Mary and Nicky popped in.

Nicky looked so grown up I hardly recognised her. It made me realise just how long I had been away. Could I return to my life again? I thought I wanted to, but was it possible after so long I wondered. That was a big issue which I thought a lot about. My family and friends had moved on but I had not.

We also paid a visit to Mum's grave. It was sad but so important to make the visit. I had been home and had to go to where we had laid Mum to rest so long ago. It was a very successful day. I felt very tired when we arrived back at the unit, but it was this the first hint that maybe, just maybe, I could once again live a normal life. Everyone was so proud of my achievements. It was so nice to feel that things were going in the right direction.

My days in the unit were long once I was getting better, but Monday to Friday was full of therapies.

By now I was beginning to venture out on my own. The therapies were based one floor down below the unit. My first venture on my own was to walk down the stairs myself. I was scared but knew this had to be done. Thinking back now it seems silly to be worried about a flight of stairs, but it was such a massive step at that stage. I did it and the middle floor were just so delighted with my clapping and cheering, it was such a memorable day.

Nurse Gilly was just so good with me. We just seemed to get on well. She helped me a lot with being away from the unit. Once I got use to going outside I wanted to do it more and more as I was so afraid I might get scared again and stop doing it. Not that that would happen with L still very much involved with my care.

My first time going into Morningside with L and Gilly was so special. I had not been at the shops for 2 years. Diane and Moira would send things in or the staff at the unit would get me what I needed. In Morningside there was a clothes shop and we went in and I got a stripy sweat shirt size ten. Me a size ten! My usual was a size 18+. I still have that top hanging up today, 8 years on. I just loved that top, it was so important. Diane always asks why I keep it as it will never fit me again. I know that, but it was such a hard battle to buy that top and I don't think I will ever part with it.

Elizabeth Fleming

Chapter 9

My days were filled with therapy, but the nights and weekends were long. Once I was getting better I started to fill my time with colouring in, jigsaws and on the computer. I would start a puzzle in the evening then go off to bed and in the morning it would be completed; the night shift would have done it. I had everyone doing puzzles. The unit was quite noisy at times so I would just go into the activity room and do things on the PC. The food in the unit was typical hospital food. The highlight of the week was Friday mornings. The OT made a full breakfast for staff and patients. Everyone helped and we all sat together. B loved his food and it was nice all having breakfast together.

   L went on holiday for 2 weeks and I had my program left for me. The student was in charge. I worked a lot with H and she was lovely. We went out for tea and coffee lots. That was the best bit of getting better, as we had to have a cake too. I very much missed L when she was away but I had had a good 2 weeks and lots to tell her when she got back.

The medication was slowly getting out my system. It got cut back mg by mg but slowly so I would not miss it. The drug had blocked out my ability to cry. It was nearly 2 years before I properly grieved for mum. I cried for days and days. It was as if mum had just died. It still baffles me today thinking how a tablet could change a person's life so much, but it did and I am living proof of that.

It was the PC that helped me make contact with family and friends I had lost touch with. My dad also gave me a new mobile so I could text my sisters in the evening and tell them what had happened throughout the day. The unit was a safe place and for me it was my home for now.

Another part of my therapy was to learn how to be still and quiet. This I did with D and H. The medication had made my tummy full of nerves. I shook uncontrollably inside. I had to retrain my body to relax again. Slowly and sitting in total silence and saying the three key words Came Quite Still over and over again in my head. This was very helpful and still if I get agitated today it helps me ground myself again.

It was coming up to Mum's anniversary and before I was in hospital I attended my local church each week. L asked if I would like the hospital minister to come and pray with me on the day. Yes, I thought. That would be nice. It meant although my life was not yet back home, my mind was still thinking about it. Gilly sat in with me and we prayed for Mum and my family. It was a very emotional moment but very important in my recovery. Gilly was to become a dear person in my life. She was, and still is, very well placed in her choice of work.

Things were going in the right direction. My sisters were visiting regularly and I had been home several times with different people. I was beginning to spend less and less time with L which was good, but I missed our chats. I just thought so much of her now I no longer feared the sight of her walking into the unit and sending me in the other direction to try to avoid her.

I always remember L asking me once Who Was The Most Important Person In My Life. I replied by saying everyone in my family and she asked where I was. Me, I said last and she replied by saying that I should always be first because I am the most important person in my life. I never ever thought of that but from then on I always remember this and try to put myself first. I still think of others but I must always remember I am important too.

My illness was like a journey and, yes, I hit rock bottom and, yes, it was a struggle and I would not wish anyone to go thought it, but I also learned to become a new and independent person. People said how much better I was since mum died but if I could get my mum back today I would. Because I miss her so much and I will miss her till we meet again. But at least I received the right help and I will always be thankful for that.

Chapter 10

For the first time since mum died I was starting to feel happy again. I found being happy difficult - how could I be happy without Mum? Only, being happy was not a sin but was a feeling I had to get used to once again.

I was doing so much out with the unit now. I started going on buses which was a big achievement. With L and the therapists with me nothing seemed impossible. I also started going to a rehabilitation unit for people with mental health problems. B help me achieve this again step by step until I felt confident enough to do it on my own.

As it was getting closer to my discharge from the unit we started to do more everyday tasks in Tranent, like visiting my own dentist, and attending my home church. Church life for me was, and still is, a very big part of my life.

It's funny looking back now, but for some reason my big fear was that I would not be welcomed back and accepted again. It had been nearly 3 years. Would people remember me and want me back? I need never have worried as I was welcomed back into my home life with open arms.

My sisters found it hard at first. My mum had died my dad had moved on and their sister had been taken away. When I came back it was not the sister they had known and loved but a very independent person who had learned to stand firmly on her own 2 feet, and they needed time to get used to that. We did and thankfully my family are as close as ever. My sisters are the best thing in my life these days, but remember it's still only 2005 in my story, but it is really 2013 today.

Chapter 11

As I was growing up, one of my dreams in life was to drive a car. I was fascinated when my dad and Diane drove. Watching their every move as I sat beside them. I just could not wait to be 17. After my 17th Birthday I went to my GP to ask if he thought it would be possible. Until the day I die I will never forget his answer, with a chuckle in his voice, he said "Drive? You? You are a spastic, however could you drive?" It felt as if my whole world had come to an end. I was devastated. How could that doctor be so heartless and blunt?

When I was in the unit and with my therapists, I spoke about every part of my life, from birth until where I was now. I must have spoken about my sadness with not getting my car. L must have thought why not have a go now when I was still getting lots of help and support, as I needed to have an assessment at Ashley Ainsley Hospital. After all these years of waiting, could my dream finally be about to come true? Nothing seemed to be too much for the caring staff who worked in the unit. I was so excited but apprehensive at the thought of the assessment, but I was reassured by everyone that with a little help I would achieve it. I was so excited to tell my dad and my sisters and brother-in-laws, if only my mum could see me, but I think she can; since my recovery I have all way felt her presence near.

Looking back to those days I often wondered what others thought of me. I, myself, felt I had failed as a daughter, sister, sister-in-law, aunty, niece and friend. Why had my life fallen apart so much? Why was I lashing out? Why did I not want to be with the people I loved so much? Where did it all go so badly wrong? But I now know I was not a bad person it was not all my fault. It was an illness and I needed special help to recover, which sadly took a long time in coming.

My brain is working hard today. I think this book is going to be good. This time I have not held back and covered up the bad and sad bits and I can't wait to finish it and hear what you all think of it.

I did not want to go home and live with Dad. I thought a place of my own would be nice, but it would be a challenge. Once again I got the help I needed to succeed. B and I applied for a house in Tranent. We had no idea how long this would take. It was scary for me to imagine being in my own home living a normal everyday life again because my life for so long had been in the hospital. The unit felt so safe and secure now. But I wanted to take the next step, even if it was hard to imagine at first.

Although I was well on the road to recovery, the past still lingered very strongly in my mind. Remember, I still thought my illness was all my doing. Although all my turns had stopped, I never felt completely free of them. To be perfectly honest, today there are very few days I don't think about them. But I understand now what happened. The first sign of agitation and my mind races back to the bad times, but Diane is my saviour and she reassures me that it will all be OK, but it's hard to have gone through a severe illness and to fully recover. I have learned how to live and cope with these feelings. This is such a hard thing to relive as the tears run down my face, but if it helps someone out there it will be so worthwhile

Elizabeth Fleming

Chapter 12

My driving assessment day arrived and I was feeling apprehensive and excited all in one. We took the car to the centre and with L by my side we went in. I asked L if she would come in with me and she said yes, if she were able to. The lady called my name and in we went. She asked a few questions and did a few tests with me. Then I went over to a big machine to test my hand and eye control. I felt this test was quite difficult and struggled a little. However the assessor said I did fine. It was very reassuring to see L nearby. She watched with interest as the tests were carried out. Then the lady said that was the first part and asked us to sit in the waiting room until she got the car.

Car, I thought. I really was about to have a shot at driving. I looked at L who looked a bit puzzled and said, "Oh, I'll just sit here until you come back." The thought of me driving and L sitting in the back did not appeal to L I don't think. I was up for it, and very excited to give it a try. The lady came back and said, "Let's see how you cope in a car." She turned and said to L, "You can come - just pop in the back and put your seatbelt on." L looked at me and looked quite nervous as she sat there. Afterwards she said she'd really wanted a crash-helmet and body-armour.

We got into the car and I was behind the wheel. How excited I was. But the assessor had controls too. We drove round the hospital grounds a few times. It felt so good I just loved the feeling of being in control. When we got back to the centre the assessor said that I would only need a peg to be put on the steering wheel of an automatic car. But I would have to wait for a letter telling me how I did. Poor L looked very relieved as she got out of the car. You can imagine, I was as high as a kite afterwards. I could not wait to tell everyone about my day.

Back in the car I could see how very proud L was of how I handled the assessments. That made me feel very proud and I realised that, yes, maybe with the right help I could begin to lead a normal life again. I always felt because I needed help with things I was letting myself down, but everyone needs help at some time, and people with a disability just need a wee bit extra. I was beginning to ask for help when I needed it and was trying hard to not feel I was letting myself down all the time. I was such an independent person before my life changed and I shut help out. But help is good when it's the right help.

Sad person that I am, I've always loved Cliff Richard. But I could never go to concerts or anything as I always hated big spaces and places where lots of people were. But now, with the right help, I was facing all my fears head on. L said, "How about you and I going to see Cliff at the Edinburgh castle?" Oh, I thought. Lots of people. Too busy for me. But a few days later I thought, why not? I didn't think L liked Cliff and she told me that she didn't, but that she wanted to see me enjoying things for a change. I was so excited about my first concert. This L lady went up in my estimations. How nice for someone to do that for a patient. The staff were all laughing at the thought of us going to see Cliff.

I went with Gilly for a new outfit, shoes and bag. I was so excited. The nurses did my hair and makeup and the OT made us Cliff tops. I was so excited. L came and got me and off we went, camera and all. It was a typical summer's night in Edinburgh - perishing. L said she had a blanket in case we were cold. I said no at first, as I wanted to show off my new outfit, but ten minutes later I was cuddling into the blanket and L for heat. Not that that stop us having a FAB time. What an experience. I kept pinching myself. Was I really there, watching my idol. I wonder if L realised how I felt and how she made one of my life time dreams come true.

Elizabeth Fleming

Chapter 13

Things were on track for my discharge in November 2004. By then I had my new flat in Tranent, just five minutes from my dad. I also had my care plan set up and was getting to know my key worker Jean. Jean was coming in to see me in the unit so we could get acquainted before my home coming.

I needed time to adapt to new things and people. I don't know if it's just my nature or my disability, but making a bond takes me time. My cousin was having a party and all my family were going to be there. My sisters thought it would be nice for me to come on my own because I had been away for such a long time and had not seen my aunty and uncles. This was a good plan.

Then one morning L came up very early. I was still in my nightwear. She popped her head round my door and wanted a quick word. "You're an early bird today," she said. She sat beside me and said something that I did not think I would ever hear.

She said, "Your dad has a new friend."

"Oh," I said. "Dad's got lots of friends."

"No. A lady friend."

My heart sank. I was speechless.

"Are you OK?" she asked.

"Yes," I said. "I think I will take a shower and get dressed," and went into my room.

"I'm only downstairs if you need me," L told me.

Back in my room I sat numb for a while. My dad with a lady friend? It must be a mistake. My dad just lived for my mum. To me they were made for each other. 42 years they lived for one another.

Then a nurse came and told me to get a shower and she'd make me something nice for breakfast.

"Yes. I'm just coming," I told her. My mind was so mixed up I just could not take it all in. The day seemed to last forever. I think I cried a bucket of tears that day. Although very mixed up, I was happy to still have the support of the unit. Beforehand Diane and Moira kept dropping hints about how time and people move on, but I just did not realise what they meant. Would this set me back? I had come to far to turn back but it was hard to come to terms with.

Here come the tears. I loved my dad so much and needed him to be there when I came home. He was getting older and I had missed so much precious time. I knew he still loved me and was looking forward to me coming home. What was I to do? I decided that if he was happy and I never met this person and still had my dad and he kept this part of his life separate from mine all would be fine. But that was not to be and he was intending to bring her to my cousin's party. My sister and I were to meet June at the party. I was feeling quite nervous about being away from the security of the unit as it had arranged for me to stay with a carer in my own flat after the party and return to the unit the following day.

The day before I felt very sick, but B and I were planning a trip out to Tranent to arrange my flat for my overnight stay. L was having none of my nonsense and we had to carry out the day's events. The thought of going home on a bus for 1 hour 30 minutes that day felt awful.

I was crying all day. Poor B tried to cheer me up by saying we could go and buy something for my new flat. I don't remember why, to this day, but we bought three wooden spoons. Why 3, I'll probably never recall. Still upset, we made our way to the bus. B did his very best to keep my morale up and it worked, as I think we both enjoyed each other's company. We got to Meadowbank stadium and I just felt my tummy rumble and I told B to take these spoons out quick and give me the bag and I was very sick. We reached Portobello and got off the bus. I handed the sick bag to B and we sat on the bench in the High Street. I felt rotten and B called a taxi and we returned to the unit. I never did ask what he did with the bag of sick.

Back at the unit I knew L would be unhappy. I just went straight into bed as my head was so sore. I hoped L would be away home early that day and my luck was in because she was, although I would have to face up to her the next day. I just chilled that night and had an early night as I still felt yucky. I woke up the next day and felt fine again, a Friday morning, glad I was at Balinden all morning. I thought I should get up quickly and miss L in the morning. It was a good idea and it worked. Sadly I had to return at lunch time and knew she would be looking for me. I came back and Gilly said L wanted to see me.

"Yes," I said. "I thought as much." I wonder if L will get a laughs when she reads this.

"What was yesterday about?" she asked.

"Well, I just felt sick and not well but I'm fine today and was at Balinden."

Which worked in my favour because L thought I would still be in bed that morning. "Yes, well, it's a good job you feel better today and your night away is still on I hope."

"Yes, L. I'm looking forward to seeing my family

again."

   "Ok then." She smiled and I smiled back.

   "Have a nice weekend. See you Monday if not before," I said. That was not as bad as I'd expected, thank goodness. I no longer feared L but she had helped me so much I did not want to let her or me down.

Elizabeth Fleming

Chapter 14

The night of the party had arrived. I was excited but apprehensive. What would it be like to see my dad with another woman? My sisters, brother-in laws and I sat quietly for a while in the hall, our eyes focused on the door. In came my dad and June. They sat away from us but we went and spoke to them. Never for one moment until a long time later did I give June a thought. She must have been feeling as apprehensive as we were. It was very hard as I loved my dad but I just felt worried. I enjoyed the party and seeing my relatives and I felt that I was going in the right direction for finally returning home.

   Ross came and picked me up and walked me home to stay in my new flat with a carer from my support team from home. It had been a good first time away from the unit and the following day I returned to the hospital. Everything was going well and the time for my discharge from hospital was approaching fast.

I had mixed feeling about coming home as I was coming home to a new beginning. The unit had become my home. My safe place. The place where I had rebuilt my new life. It was scary to leave, but I hoped it was the right time. The Unit made my departure easy step by step. I was going to miss the people who helped me so much. It was hard not to get attached. But I kept in touch with Gilly and L which helped very much. I still exchange the odd letter and cards at special times of the year. I meet up with Gilly sometimes. I will never forget my time spent at the unit. It was the hardest time of my life. The only words I can think of to express it are that I had been 'to Hell and back'. Looking back it is not all bad and sad. There were some good times. I will be always grateful for the help and chances I was giving to make a new and independent life for myself. No words could ever thank these caring special people who took care and looked after me for 2 years and 6 months of my life.

Finally the 29th November 2004 came - the day of my discharge. I woke up excited and was scared what lay ahead of me. I suppose in some way I never thought this day would come. L had not got in that morning and in some ways I was glad as how could I say goodbye. Although I knew we would keep in touch, how could I ever say thank you for saving my life? L always said it was me who did the hard work and yes it was, but she was with me each step of the way. I will never forget the help she gave me. L always said she would never forget me and I certainly will never forget her. I still find it hard to believe I could dislike a person so much and then look up to that same person.

A, the OT, took me home. My heart was heavy when we said goodbye, but I still had contact with everyone for the first few months. Here I was sitting in my own flat by myself for the first time in 2 years 6 months. Another thing that helped was my bed in the unit was kept for 8 weeks just in case things did not work out, but luckily I never needed it.

We are now in June 2012. It's hard to say how long my story might take to complete. I am very much enjoying my writing. If only I had more time. It's like making a journey through my past life. Reliving my past is hard, but it is amazing to see how far my life has changed.

Elizabeth Fleming

Chapter 15

Being home was good and I seemed to settle into my new life quickly. Everything was set in place and I had people coming in and out regularly which helped. I just loved my wee flat. It was so good to have my own space.

I was to get a home help, the first day she arrived, she came in and said, "Nice to meet you Liz Fleming," and I told her my name was Elizabeth and that is what I would like to be called. My mum was called Liz and hearing her name still hurt. Maureen though, well I like a challenge and I was her first client in her new job. We were to become such good friends I often said I thought my mum picked Maureen and sent her to help me settle in to my life at home.

We had a nice Christmas my first year home. I spent Christmas Eve with my dad and Christmas Day with my family. I had missed my family and the children so much. They had all grown up. Ross had come into hospital on many occasions but my nieces were still quite young. As I sat round the Christmas table that year I was home but still wondered if I would fit in to my much loved family. My sisters must have had their thoughts. It all seems so long ago and I never thought I would find the happiness and love we had before Mum died. Although once you lose your mum nothing is quite the same, but we three sisters are closer now than ever before.

My flat was nice and cosy. When people came in they would say it had a warm and welcoming feeling. I had a review and my therapists came from the Unit. I was so delighted to see everyone again. I loved my home life but I missed everyone from the unit, and I knew the time was coming to say my final goodbyes. Everyone was delighted with my progress. Things were going very well and I was getting ready to begin my lessons so I could get my long awaited car.

My confidence was very high and I felt I could face my next challenge. I was very excited about my driving and could not wait to begin. My first instructor was not very good so I moved to British School Of Motoring. This time it was a lady and she was very patient with me.

Although up to that point of my life I never felt my CP held me back from anything I wanted to do, I was also very realistic and knew if I ever was to succeed it would take me a lot longer. Everything from my birth to the present day has taken me longer but there are not a lot of things I set out to do that have beaten me. The only thing that got the better of me was roller skates; I just did not have the balance. That's not too bad in 45 years.

Elizabeth Fleming

Chapter 16

My friends.

   After my discharge from hospital, my fear was whether I could have my old friends back again. Life for me had stood still for nearly three years. Could I pick up the pieces with my friends? Sadly the answer was no. Although Mary Ann and Leona all visited me in hospital, once I was home our friendships did not last. I was sad especially with Mary. We shared a life-long friendship and I really miss her. I still miss our friendship today. I sit here with tears running down my face and wondering if Mary ever knew how much she meant to me.

   I was lucky because once home I had my church family. The 2 most important people in my church family are my dear and much loved friends Ellen and Sam. They came and took me out for dinners from the unit. Ellen is just so kind and caring. She is always there with her special ways. Sam's my handy man. If something breaks I just give him a call and he comes with tools in hand. They both mean so much to me, although I forget to tell them that sometimes.

My home help Maureen was to become such a loyal and special person. It is so hard to put into words how much I treasure her. Yes, she helped me with household tasks, but with so much more as well. Throughout those seven years we grew so close. We shared laughter and tears. We went out to theatre and for meals. We so much enjoyed each other's company. She was just the best friend anyone could have asked for.

I have made lots of new friends in church, or should I say my church family. My church life is so important to me. I just can't wait for Sunday mornings. Every one of my church friends is precious, but Janice, Judith and Cath are extra special. We ladies have become close and are around the same age. We are all going through middle age and how much I appreciate having people who understand what I am going through.

Chapter 17

Once all my care was working and set in place, it was the time to start my driving lessons. I was excited and nervous but felt positive with the right instructor who was very understanding and took it at my pace so I could achieve my goal.

Unfortunately the first instructor was not for me. He was not very understanding. It put me off for a time but then I got a lady instructor and this was to work out very well.

  It took me just under 2 years and three attempts to pass my driving test. My dad's friend, June, was the only one to take me to practice my driving. I will always be grateful for the help she gave me. I was on Cloud 9 the day I passed. Never in my wildest dreams did I ever think I could achieve passing my driving test. This was for certain my biggest achievement. Nothing in this life is impossible with the right help. Where was that doctor who said to me "You're a spastic. How could you every drive?" I certainly proved him wrong.

I was now able to go out on my own. I wonder if you can think where my first drive on my own was. It was to my mum's grave. Well Mum had to be the first one on my list to tell. How PROUD everyone was of me. I received over 50 cards. The unit staff was so happy. If it had not been for L's therapies I might not have lived my dream. It was to be the happiest time of my whole life.

If only my mum could have seen me. Although Mum's not here in body, she's always here in my heart. Time passes and people die, but no one can every take the past away and the special memories we once shared. I believe that my time will come when we meet again. Oh what joy will fill my heart. There was a time in the black days when I wanted it to come, but now I am so glad to have come through these times. I so very much value life when I spend precious time with the third generation of my own family. I have to stop now as the tears are falling onto my PC.

Having a car and my freedom was the best. I could do anything I wanted. I wondered how long this happiness would last.

Chapter 18

Being out of hospital was good, although it was hard to move on as my life for 3 years had been so different. I was so happy to be back in the place where I belonged. Church was, and still is, a big part of my life.

I was heading for my fortieth and wanted a party. At this time I was beginning to feel my Cerebral Palsy was beginning to affect me. My hand coordination was giving me some pain and I had terrible pain in my lower back. I went to my GP who at that time said it was muscular and prescribed me Paracetamol which was no help.

They say life begins at forty. For me this was not to be the case. From my back pain to my hand pain I now had to adapt to a new stage in my life. I suppose I should have counted myself lucky to have Cerebral Palsy since birth and no pain, but it was so hard as I do not have a very high pain threshold. It has taken over the last 6 years of my life.

I spent the first 2 years 6 months in and out of doctors', physiotherapists' and consults' waiting rooms, with no glimmers of a diagnosis or any pain relief. My dad paid for me to go for private treatment. We must have spent close to a £1000 pounds with no help to gain from it. I was in total agony. They kept saying it was my CP. How could this be, that after nearly forty years of having no pain. I could hardly walk, wash or dress myself or do my own hair or make a cooked meal. It was awful. The last straw came when I was referred to a pain management team. The medical profession had run out of ideas and thought it was all in my head. My family was beginning to have doubts. Was it in my head? Could I really be imagining pain? You could see in my face that this was taking over my life. However, I had to give it a try. They were trying to teach me how to think of something nice and breathe though the pain. However after 2 years 6 months a physiotherapist suggested a MIR but thought with my Cerebral Palsy I might not be able to keep still. I said yes. Anything, even if I had to be sedated it was worth a go.

I went for my MIR scan, not the nicest of things I might add, but with Diane by my side I managed to keep still. At long last, 2 year 6 months, later we got the answer I was waiting for. It was not all in my head after all. My discs were crumbling away from the bottom of my spine. I needed a 5 hour op to try and take the pain away. There was no guarantee it would work, but leaving it undone was not an option.

I was admitted to the RIH on the beginning of August 2010. I had to be in at 7.30am and did not go down to theatre until 1.30pm. It was the longest morning of my life. I was quite apprehensive beforehand as I did not realise just how long it was going to take. I did not get back to the ward until just before midnight. I am very hard to wake up after an anesthetic. Again, I put my loved ones through another worrying time.

Elizabeth Fleming

Chapter 19

I left hospital 5 days later still in a great deal of pain, with not much after-care. Thank goodness for my family and friends. All was going fine until 3 weeks later and out of the blue my Dad suddenly passed away. Ross found him on a Tuesday morning. He was not very well on the Monday and Diane called the GP in to see him. The GP said he seemed a bit chesty but he was fine, but that was not the case. Something told me that morning that all was not well. I had a gut feeling, so instead of waiting for help I just got myself ready. I phoned my carer to come and take me up to my dad's, but we were all too late. Our much-loved Dad died without any one by his side. He was quite a stubborn man and was very set in his ways. Diane said she wanted to stay over that night, but my dad said a good night's sleep was all he needed for him to be fine in the morning.

It was such a shock. If only we had known. The signs were there, but it was too late. My dad had gone. Mum's death was long and painful, but we had the time to say goodbye. Dad's was so sudden it was better for him, but much harder for the ones left behind. We had to wait 2 weeks as they took his body for a Post Mortem Waiting was hard but we got through it somehow. Diane, Moira and I have to live with the thought of him dying alone. I feel so sad no one was with him, but the paramedics assured us it was instant. There was a broken glass on the bedroom floor and they said he must have leaned over for a drink and died instantly. That helped a bit, but I still wish we had been with him.

My recovery from my back surgery had to be rushed as I did not want to go to Dad's funeral with a Zimmer frame. I think, looking back, I rushed my recovery. Diane, Moira and I felt very alone. We were orphans.

My operation had taken a lot out of me and my Cerebral Palsy was getting worse. After 6 weeks I was once again washing and dressing myself. I was finding this task very hard. People were beginning to notice my hair was not as nice and I looked a bit untidy. I was very exhausted and my back was very sore. In May 2011 we called the care team to asses my needs. Once I started to tell the lady how things were it was decided that I needed carers in the morning for personnel care. I was very upset. Although I have a disability I was never made to feel any different from my friends or family. My parents treated me the same way they treated my sisters. I felt a failure. I knew old people from church got help, but me? I was only 42. It just felt wrong.

If I put people's names in my book it is because I have their permission.

However I need not have worried as the ladies were so kind. My new carers were Diane Muriel and Melina. They were very caring and realised it would take me a bit of time getting used to them. Once we settled into a new routine, everything was fine.

Life, once again, was a struggle as I no longer had my dad. I grieved the proper way this time. Moira found Dad's death hard to cope with. I found myself trying to help her through this difficult time.

Elizabeth Fleming

Chapter 20

About three years ago I was beginning to feel a little fed-up sitting in the house. My dad was always popping in and out but I no longer had this. Although my back still hurt I though surely I could find something. I contacted my local back-to-work group and was allocated a key worker called Gary. We both wondered what I would I like to do. I had only ever worked with children and although it was very rewarding it was also very hard work.

"What about old people?" Gary said.

"I'm not too fond of old dears."

"What about office work?"

"Yes, but my spelling is not very good."

A place came up at an old people's home in Tranent. I was not convinced it was for me, but I thought I would give it a go. I went a few times, but I did not enjoy it.

"What about a school?"

"Yes, that's more like it for me."

There was a voluntary job delivering fruit to P1 and P2. This was more like it. I have been at the school for over 2 years. I very much enjoy the company. The staff and children are just lovely. It was there that I got my first book published. One of the support teachers is a writer and we got speaking and he asked to see my story. He was able to get it published as an E-book. I was very excited to have a book published. Hopefully I might be lucky and get the next one published too.

At the end of 2011 my dear and much loved friend Maureen died. Her cancer had returned, but this time it was very aggressive. Watching her die was so painful. We had become so very close. She passed away on the 11th December. I was heart-broken. I love Christmas but I just could not put my tree up that year. Oh how I miss her, but I thank God for all the lovely times and memories we shared.

At the beginning 2012 June, my key worker for 8 years, left the support team. I had grown very close to Jean in the previous 8 years. Maureen's death and Jean leaving was a big gap in my life. I find change very hard to cope with. I like my routine.

Chapter 21

As the years go on, I feel sometimes my mental health is neglected. Because I seem to be coping fine, my carers forget the real reason why my care is provided. When Jean left I feel there should have been a new carer to replace her. Sadly this was not to be the case and it was a case of whoever was on the shift came. I am quite a private person and it takes me a long time to build up relationships with people. Some carers think you can tell all staff members the same. In the staff team who support me there are between 10 and15 people. It's not fair that you are expected to trust everyone the same. Since my discharge from hospital until a few months ago things were fine. But I am looking to change my support as it is no longer meeting my needs.

I am coming very close to ending my second book. There are so many people I would love to name but I would be here forever. I hope the people I have not written about are not too upset, because you are all very special and in one way or other you have enhanced my life, be it big or small. I have decided to be very secretive about this book. Up until now only my dear friend Gilly has read part of it as she could not wait until it was finished.

I would also like to thank my publisher Nigel. I hope my second book with be as popular as the first.

If you're purchasing any of my books feel free to comment on them – it's so nice for people to tell me what they think of my books. My first book has just been put into paperback. To see a book with my face on the cover is the best.

What would my mum and dad think of me? I still miss them more and more with each new day. But they left their strength and love which help me and my much loved family help me to face each new hurdle in life one day at a time.

Chapter 22

This piece of writing is about how I now face each day with my Cerebral Palsy.

Up until I hit forty I could say, yes I had a disability, but I never felt it held me back for doing anything I wanted to achieve. But since I hit forty it has been a different story. I was quit looking forward to becoming forty. Age has never bothered me, but the aches and pains that came with it do. I wonder and so wish someone could tell me why my body hurts so much. Is it my CP or is it just getting older. For 6 years I have lived in pain. I am on the strongest pain relief, but still it throbs on. I have a super GP at the moment, which is a great help. Myself with Dr S have looked for specialist CP consultants.

If you are a child from birth to 17 you can receive all the treatment you need. I have never been seen by a specialist doctor for my condition since the age of 13 years old. 34 years of wondering and thinking is it my disability or just my body aging? If there is anyone out there who knows of anyone please let me know? Until then my GP and I will just have to keep looking.

Chapter 23

The family

Diane and Moira are just the best sisters you could ask for (not that I tell them that in case it might make them big headed). Since mum and dad died we have grown much closer. We really only have each other. To lose both parents is very hard. I used to say to people how hard it was, but until you have to live though it you really don't understand. If, like us, you have had the best mum and dad the pain never goes away. Yes, time eases the pain but inside there is a hole that no one or anything can fill. It must be hard not to have a family or be an only child.

John and Derek are my 2 brother-in-laws. They feel just like the brothers I never had. They help me with men's work. I love being with them. John came into the Unit and helped me to face the outside world again.

The children have turned into fine young adults.

They have all made their way in the world and I am very proud aunty. We now have the next generation. I wonder what their lives will be like. I can't wait to watch them grow.

Other Sea Minor titles include:

With A Little Help From My Friends by Elizabeth
Fleming

My Friend Miranda by IM Griffin

a Sea Minor Publication

© 2013

15711631R00053

Printed in Great Britain
by Amazon